J612

KU-863-064

1/96

MSC

SCHOOLS LIBRARY SERVICE
Maltby Library Headquarters
High Street
Maltby
Rotherham S66 8LA

ROTHERHAM PUBLIC LIBRARIES

This book must be returned by the date specified at the time of
issue as the Date Due for Return.
The loan may be extended (personally, by post or telephone) for
a further period, if the book is not required by another reader,
by quoting the above number   LM1 (C)

ROTHERHAM
PUBLIC LIBRARIES

J612

411 823 6

53142

SCHOOLS STOCK

Acknowledgements

Educational consultant Viv Edwards, Professor of
Language in Education, University of Reading.
Photographs by Zul Mukhida except for:
p. 2t John Heinrich, p. 5b Graham Horner, p. 7 John Heinrich,
p. 12b Graham Horner, p. 19 John Heinrich, Zul Colour
Library; pp. 1b, 15r Peter Sanders Photography; pp. 3, 8r, 14
Sporting Pictures (UK) Ltd; p. 5t John Birdsall Photography;
p. 12t Sally & Richard Greenhill Photo Library;
p. 18 Eamonn McNulty/Science Photo Library.

The author and publisher would like to thank: the staff and
pupils of Balfour Infant School, Brighton; Nahib and Jessica;
Richard Vobes, mime; Simon Hart.

A CIP catalogue record for this book is available
from the British Library.

ISBN 0-7136-4241-6

First published 1995 by A & C Black (Publishers) Ltd
35 Bedford Row, London WC1R 4JH

© 1995 A & C Black (Publishers) Ltd

All rights reserved. No part of this publication may be
reproduced or used in any form or by any means – graphic,
electronic or mechanical, including photocopying, recording,
taping or information storage and retrieval systems – without
the prior permission in writing of the publishers.

Typeset in 15/21pt Univers Medium by
Rowland Phototypesetting Ltd, Bury St Edmunds, Suffolk.

Printed in France by Partenaires

The body

Nicola Edwards

A&C Black · London

You can sometimes see messages on people's bodies.

These Aboriginal dancers have painted their faces and bodies. In their dance they pretend to be different animals.

The guests at this Muslim wedding have painted the bride's hands with henna. Henna is a special dye that comes from a plant.

These football fans have painted
their faces in their team's colours.

People use their bodies to send
messages to each other.

This police officer is using his arms
and hands to control the traffic.

These deaf people are using their hands to talk to each other. This is called sign language.

This conductor is using his arms and hands to guide the musicians in the orchestra.
His movements tell the musicians when to play their instruments and how loud to play them.

Movements of the body can mean different things.

How are the people in these pictures using their bodies to say hello to each other?

Can you think of other ways of greeting people with your body?

Why do you think these people
are waving?

People can use their bodies
to show they are happy . . .

. . . or that they need
cheering up.

Look at the children
in these pictures.
Which parts of their
bodies are they using?
How do you think
they are feeling?

Sometimes you can tell how people are feeling just by looking at their faces.

Can you describe how these children are feeling?

We can make different noises with our bodies.

Babies cry to let people know they are hungry or that their nappies need changing.

These women are using their voices to sing in a choir.

Can you guess what sort of noises
the children in these pictures
are making?

13

Sometimes crowds of
people move together
in the same way
to send a message.

The people in this
crowd are watching
a game of football.
They show they are
enjoying themselves
by joining in a
'Mexican wave'.

These followers of the Muslim religion are taking part in prayers at a mosque.

We find out about the world around us through touch, taste, smell, hearing and sight. These are called the five senses.

How are these children using their five senses?

17

When people are ill, their bodies can show signs which help doctors discover what is wrong.

This girl is feeling poorly. She feels hot and so a doctor is taking her temperature.

These people are wearing hats and using sun cream to protect themselves while they sunbathe. How can a body show if a person has been in the hot sun for too long?

Our bodies show we are
growing up . . .

. . . and growing older.

People can use their bodies to tell stories without words.

This mime artist is acting out a story without speaking. What do you think he is telling you?

These dancers are moving their bodies to music to tell a story.

What sort of movements would you make to show that you are angry, sad or excited?

23

Index

For parents and teachers

The aim of the *Messages* series is to help build confidence in children who are just beginning to read, by encouraging them to make meaning from the different kinds of signs and symbols which surround them in their everyday lives. Here are some suggestions for follow-up activities which extend the ideas introduced in the book.

Pages 2/3 Some children may be able to describe the experience of having their faces painted to make them look like animals or perhaps Halloween characters. You could talk about how make-up is used to transform a person's appearance and show the children 'before and after' photographs of, for example, a young actor made up to look like an old person. Some of the children may have been to a Muslim wedding or have a relative whom you could invite into school to show the children how the intricate henna patterns are applied to women's hands and feet on special occasions, particularly weddings.

Pages 4/5 Ask the children to think about the journey they make from home to school and the different ways in which they may see people communicating with each other using gestures, for example, a lollipop person stopping traffic and signalling to pedestrians that it is safe to cross the road. You could read the children an account written by a deaf person describing what it is like to be deaf – there are several books available which are aimed specifically at young children.

Pages 6/7 Ask the children about the ways in which they use their bodies to say hello and goodbye to different people: for example, how do they greet their schoolteacher in the morning? How is it different from the way in which they would greet a member of their family? There are opportunities to explore the variety of gestures used in different cultures.

Pages 8/9 Collect pictures from newspapers and magazines of people in different postures displaying a variety of emotions. The children could pick one each and use it as a starting point for a story, perhaps ending at the moment at which the photograph was taken.

Pages 10/11 Divide the children into two groups; ask the first group to use their faces to show a series of different emotions for the other group to guess (the groups could take turns at acting and guessing).

Pages 12/13 Play the children a tape of different sounds made by the body, such as footsteps, handclaps, tap-dancing, whistling or laughing, and ask them to guess what each of the sounds are.

Pages 14/15 You could play a game of 'Simon says' with younger children to demonstrate how a group of people can move their bodies in unison. Older children could work on a group dance to express, for example, how waves swell and crash onto a beach. Talk about how people from different religions use their bodies to express devotion to God, such as kneeling, genuflecting, bowing heads or prostrating their bodies.

Pages 16/17 Ask a child to identify a series of small objects with their eyes closed, using touch, smell, hearing and, where appropriate, taste. Finally, let the child see the objects. Which sense, or combination of senses, is the most useful in each case? This could lead to a discussion of the ways in which blind people have to rely on their remaining senses.

Pages 18/19 Some of the children may be able to talk about what it was like to have an illness such as chickenpox. You could invite a local doctor or nurse into school to talk to the children about their work in a hospital and the different ways of discovering why a person is feeling unwell using, for instance, thermometers, x-rays or stethoscopes.

Pages 20/21 The children may be able to bring in their local authority health record books which will show how their height and weight have changed as they have grown older. Photographs of family members could be used to make a family tree showing different generations and ages.

Pages 22/23 You could organise an outing to a performance by a local dance troupe or invite a mime artist into school to perform for the children and perhaps talk to them afterwards and answer their questions. The children could then try miming their interpretation of different emotions or situations which you suggest to them.